A Little Night Music

Music and Lyrics by Stephen Sondheim

Book by Hugh Wheeler

Suggested by a Film by Ingmar Bergman

Live dramatic performance rights for "A Little Night Music" are represented exclusively by
Music Theatre International (MTI)
421 West 54th St., New York, NY 10019
www.MTIshows.com
For further information, please call (212) 541-4684
or email: Licensing@MTIshows.com.

ISBN 978-1-4234-8628-2

RILTING MUSIC, INC.

EXCLUSIVELY DISTRIBUTED BY

7777 W. BLUEMOUND RD. P.O. BOX 13819 MILWAUKEE, WI 53213

Visit Hal Leonard Online at
www.halleonard.com

STEPHEN SONDHEIM wrote the music and lyrics for *Road Show* (2008), *Passion* (1994), *Assassins* (1991), *Into the Woods* (1987), *Sunday in the Park with George* (1984), *Merrily We Roll Along* (1981), *Sweeney Todd* (1979), *Pacific Overtures* (1976), *The Frogs* (1974), *A Little Night Music* (1973), *Follies* (1971, revised in London, 1987), *Company* (1970), *Anyone Can Whistle* (1964), and *A Funny Thing Happened on the Way to the Forum* (1962), as well as lyrics for *West Side Story* (1957), *Gypsy* (1959), *Do I Hear A Waltz?* (1965), and additional lyrics for *Candide* (1973). *Side by Side by Sondheim* (1976), *Marry Me A Little* (1981), *You're Gonna Love Tomorrow* (1983), and *Putting It Together* (1992) are anthologies of this work as a composer and lyricist. For films, he composed the scores of *Stavisky* (1974) and *Reds* (1981) and songs for *Dick Tracy* (1990), for which he won an Academy Award. He also wrote songs for the television production "Evening Primrose" (1966), co-authored the film *The Last of Sheila* (1973) and the play *Getting Away With Murder* (1996), and provided incidental music for the plays *The Girls of Summer* (1956), *Invitation to a March* (1961), and *Twigs* (1971). He won Tony Awards for Best Score for a Musical for *Passion, Into the Woods, Sweeney Todd, A Little Night Music, Follies,* and *Company.* All of these shows won the New York Drama Critics Circle Award, as did *Pacific Overtures* and *Sunday in the Park with George,* the latter also receiving the Pulitzer Prize for Drama (1985). He received a special 2008 Tony Award for Lifetime Achievement in the Theatre. Mr. Sondheim was born in 1930 and raised in New York City. He graduated from Williams College, winning the Hutchinson Prize for Music Composition, after which he studied theory and composition with Milton Babbitt. He is on the Council of the Dramatists Guild, the national association of playwrights, composers, and lyricists, having served as its president from 1973 to 1981, and in 1983 was elected to the American Academy of Arts and Letters. In 1990 he was appointed the first Visiting Professor of Contemporary Theatre at Oxford University and in 1993 was a recipient of the Kennedy Center Honors.

Contents

8   Now

20   Later

26   Soon

32   Remember?

35   You Must Meet My Wife

40   Liaisons

54   In Praise of Women

62   Every Day a Little Death

72   Night Waltz

76   It Would Have Been Wonderful

86   Send in the Clowns

90   The Miller's Son

96   The Glamorous Life (Film Version)

A LITTLE NIGHT MUSIC

Music and Lyrics by Stephen Sondheim
Book by Hugh Wheeler
Suggested by a film by Ingmar Bergman
Originally Produced and Directed on Broadway by Harold Prince

A Little Night Music, inspired by Bergman's 1956 film, *Smiles of a Summer Night*, was best described by Sondheim as "whipped cream with knives." The score is a series of variations on ¾ time, appropriate not only for the Old World setting, but for the various love triangles. Like Sondheim's prior shows with Prince, *Company* and *Follies*, it is smart, stylish, and refreshingly frank. It was a critical and popular success, won a slew of awards, and yielded the standard, "Send in the Clowns," recorded by Judy Collins, Frank Sinatra, and over 400 others. Having been produced the world over in theatres and opera houses, *A Little Night Music* continues to be a modern classic.

Major Productions

Broadway, Shubert Theatre,
transferred to the Majestic Theatre, 1973
Starring Glynis Johns, Hermione Gingold, Len Cariou
Directed by Harold Prince
6 Tony Awards, including Best Musical,
Best Score, Best Book
6 Drama Desk Awards, including Outstanding
Musical, Outstanding Music, Outstanding Lyrics,
Outstanding Book

London West End, Adelphi Theatre, 1975
Starring Jean Simmons, Hermione Gingold,
Joss Ackland
Directed by Harold Prince

Film Version, New World Pictures, 1978
Starring Elizabeth Taylor, Hermione Gingold,
Len Cariou
Directed by Harold Prince
Academy Award for Best Score

New York City Opera, 1990, 2003
Starring Sally Ann Howes, Regina Resnick, George
Lee Andrews (1990); Juliet Stevenson, Claire Bloom,
Jeremy Irons (2003)
Directed by Scott Ellis
Broadcast on PBS Live at Lincoln Center, 1990

London, Royal National Theatre, 1995
Starring Judi Dench, Sian Phillips, Laurence Guittard
Directed by Sean Mathias

London, Menier Chocolate Factory, 2008,
transferred to London West End, Garrick Theatre,
2009, transferred to Broadway (see below)
Starring Hannah Waddingham, Maureen Lipman,
Alexander Hanson
Directed by Trevor Nunn

Broadway, Walter Kerr Theatre, 2009
Starring Catherine Zeta-Jones (succeeded by Bernadette Peters), Angela Lansbury (succeeded by Elaine Stritch), Alexander Hanson
Directed by Trevor Nunn

Recordings

Original Broadway Cast Album, Columbia (now Sony Masterworks Broadway), 1973 (re-mastered CD, 1998)
Grammy Award, Best Musical Show Album, 1973
Grammy Award, Song of the Year ("Send in the Clowns"), 1975

Original London Cast Album, RCA (now Sony Masterworks Broadway), 1975 (CD, 1990)

Film Soundtrack Recording, Columbia, 1978 (LP and cassette only)

UK Studio Cast Album, Jay/TER Records, 1990/1996

Royal National Theatre Cast Album, Tring Records, 1997

Broadway Revival Cast Album, Nonesuch/PS Classics, 2010

Video

Film Version 1978 / Henstooth Video DVD 2007

Plot Synopsis

by Sean Patrick Flahaven

It's midsummer in turn-of-the-(last)-century Sweden. A quintet enters and begins to vocalize. They are joined in a waltz by the rest of the cast, with everyone changing partners (**Overture** and **Night Waltz**). They exit, and the elderly and imperious Madame Armfeldt enters in a wheelchair pushed by Frid, her butler. She is at her country estate and is accompanied by her precocious 13-year-old granddaughter, Fredrika. Mme. Armfeldt plays solitaire on her lap desk. Fredrika begins to question her and we learn of Mme. Armfeldt's disdain for Fredrika's absent mother, an actress.

The scene shifts to the home of lawyer Fredrik Egerman. His son, Henrik, a 19-year-old seminary student, is practicing the cello, while Henrik's pretty, 18-year-old stepmother, Anne, teases him for his gloominess and repression. Fredrik arrives home for tea-time and surprises a delighted Anne with tickets to the theatre: a French comedy starring the well-known actress Desirée Armfeldt. Fredrik retires to nap, but secretly hopes to finally, after 11 months, bed his still-virgin wife (**Now**). Henrik, infatuated with Anne, is taunted by Petra, the saucy maid, who playfully turns away his advances. He plays the cello and laments his fate (**Later**). Anne prattles and promises that she'll acquiesce to Fredrik…**Soon**. Fredrik, resigned, drifts to sleep, murmuring "Desirée," which doesn't escape Anne's notice.

Back in the country, Fredrika reads letters from her mother, Desirée, and idolizes her itinerant artist lifestyle. Desirée and the quintet go through the motions of a troupe of touring second-rate actors (**The Glamorous Life**).

Later, at the theatre, Fredrik and Anne watch the performance of *Woman of the World*. When Desirée makes her entrance and spies Fredrik, the action freezes and the quintet gives voice to their reminiscence (**Remember?**). When the action resumes, Anne, sensing that Desirée and Fredrik have some past connection, storms out, pursued by Fredrik. They arrive home, nearly interrupting Henrik's failed attempt to make love to an amused Petra. Anne is jealous, but only succeeds in making Fredrik feel old. When she goes to bed, he goes for a walk.

Fredrik arrives at Desirée's digs, surprising her. They flirt and recall their affair of 14 years ago. Desirée gently mocks him and describes her latest lover, a stupid and jealous dragoon. Fredrik insists that **You Must Meet My Wife**, but she is horrified that Anne has refused to consummate the marriage. They retire to the bedroom to make love.

In the interlude, Mme. Armfeldt recalls her long line of lovers (**Liaisons**) and then falls asleep.

Fredrik and Desirée are post-coital when the pompous dragoon, Count Carl-Magnus Malcolm arrives, on leave from the cavalry. They fabricate an excuse that Fredrik is her mother's lawyer and was bringing papers for her to sign, when he fell in the hip-bath and soaked his clothes, hence his state of undress. Fredrik hustles out, leaving Carl-Magnus to brood over what really happened (**In Praise of Women**).

Later, at home, the Count informs Charlotte, his long-suffering, cynical wife, that he has only five hours' leave to spend with her. He angrily describes his encounter with Fredrik—Charlotte knows about his affair with Desirée—and insists that she visit Anne, the younger sister of her school friends, to tattle on Fredrik. She reluctantly agrees.

Charlotte arrives at the Egerman house and her small talk with Anne quickly turns to an emotional breakdown as she reveals her passionate frustration with Carl-Magnus and both men's affair with Desirée. Anne is shocked and they bemoan their philandering husbands (**Every Day a Little Death**). Charlotte departs and Henrik attempts to comfort Anne.

Back in the country, Mme. Armfeldt is playing solitaire again while dispensing advice to Fredrika. Desirée arrives and suggests that her mother invite the Egermans to visit. Mme. Armfeldt grudgingly acquiesces and invitations are sent (**A Weekend in the Country**).

Act Two begins (**The Sun Won't Set**). Mme. Armfeldt holds court on the lawn with Desirée and Fredrika. They are interrupted by the early arrival of Carl-Magnus and Charlotte, uninvited, who run into Fredrik, Anne, Henrik, and Petra. Desirée tries to hold herself together and attempts to diffuse the tension (**Night Waltz II**). In the garden, Anne and Charlotte plot together. Charlotte suggests that she will make love to Fredrik, which will drive Carl-Magnus back to her out of jealousy, and drive Desirée away from Fredrik. Anne, naïvely confused, agrees. In another part of the garden, Henrik unburdens his frustrations to prematurely wise Fredrika.

On the terrace, Fredrik and Carl-Magnus face off (**It Would Have Been Wonderful**) and both steal a private moment with Desirée, who favors Fredrik. Dinner is served, and the quintet observes the repressed anxieties of the guests (**Perpetual Anticipation**). Charlotte, drunk, throws herself at Fredrik; Carl-Magnus becomes jealous and more pompous; and Henrik makes a scene attempting to defend Anne's innocence. Mme. Armfeldt dismisses the foolishness and toasts, "To Life! And to the only other reality—Death!"

In the garden after dinner, Henrik, ashamed, tells Fredrika he is going to kill himself. Fredrika tells Anne about Henrik's secret feelings for her, prompting Anne to run after him.

In another part of the garden, Frid and Petra mock the rich, get drunk, and make love on the soft grass.

In her bedroom, Desirée makes a sincere attempt to win Fredrik's love but is bittersweetly rebuffed (**Send in the Clowns**).

Back in the garden, Anne catches up to Henrik, who has bungled hanging himself. He professes his love to her, and they kiss. Elsewhere, Frid has fallen asleep after having sex, and Petra debates marrying **The Miller's Son**.

Fredrik, searching for Anne, instead finds Charlotte, who apologizes for her earlier behavior. While they look on in shock, Henrik and Anne, enraptured with each other, make plans to leave together.

In her bedroom, Desirée is fending off Carl-Magnus's advances when he spies Fredrik and Charlotte through the window and assumes the worst.

Mme. Armfeldt, impressed by Fredrika's perceptions of the follies of the guests, tells her about her first lover.

Carl-Magnus, furious, challenges Fredrik to a game of Russian roulette, to Charlotte's horror and delight. Fredrik is resigned and goes along. Desirée arrives too late – the gun goes off – but Carl-Magnus, disgusted, drags Fredrik back, explaining that he somehow managed merely to graze his ear. Charlotte, happy that Carl-Magnus finally "became a tiger" for her, departs with him.

Fredrik awakens and tells Desirée about Henrik and Anne. He comes to his senses, laughs at himself and embraces Desirée (**Reprises**).

Fredrika says that she hasn't yet seen the night smile. Mme. Armfeldt tells her that it has already smiled for the young and the fools: "The smile for the fools was particularly broad tonight." It smiles for the old, and Mme. Armfeldt dies. The music swells and everyone dances with their new partners in a last waltz (**Last Waltz**).

NOW

Music and Lyrics by
STEPHEN SONDHEIM

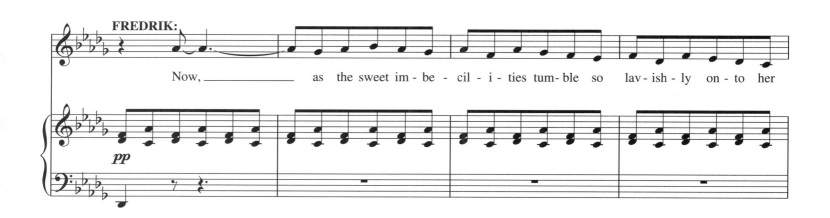

FREDRIK:

Now, _____ as the sweet im - be - cil - i - ties tum - ble so lav - ish - ly on - to her lap...

ANNE: *(spoken)* Oh, Fredrik, what a day it's been!   *Unending drama! While Petra was brushing my hair,*

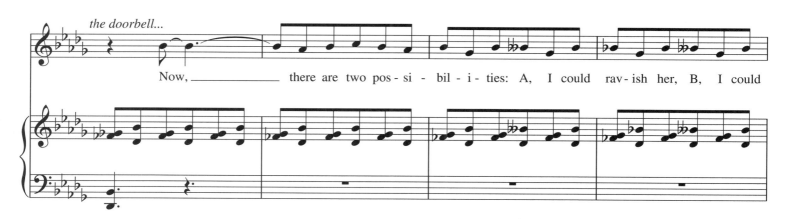

the doorbell...

Now, _____ there are two pos - si - bil - i - ties: A, I could rav - ish her, B, I could

take me all day And her sub - se - quent loath - ing would turn me a - way, Which e -

lim - i - nates B and which leaves us with A.

ANNE: *(spoken) Could you ever be jealous*

of me?

Now, _____ in so far as ap -

ANNE: *(spoken) Shall I learn Italian?*

proach - ing it, What would be fes - tive But have its ef - fect?

I think it would be amusing, if the verbs aren't too irregular.

Now, _____ there are two ways of broach-ing it: A, the sug - ges - tive and B, the di -

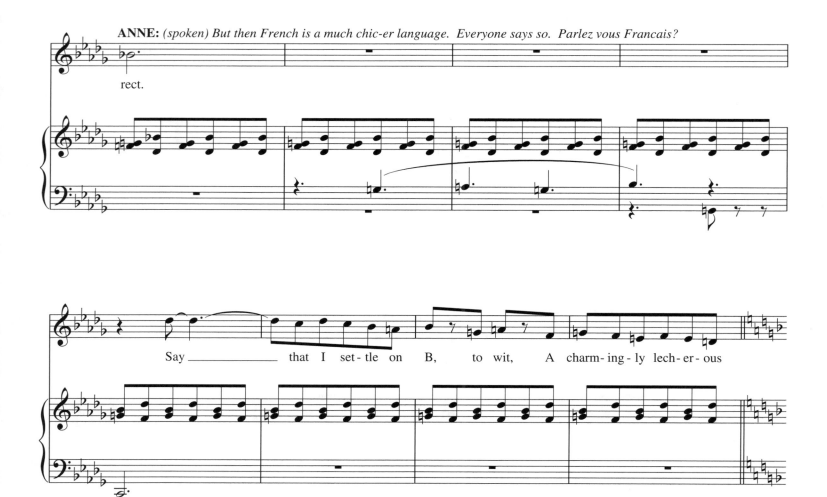

rect.

ANNE: *(spoken) But then French is a much chic-er language. Everyone says so. Parlez vous Francais?*

Say _____ that I set - tle on B, to wit, A charm - ing - ly lech - er - ous

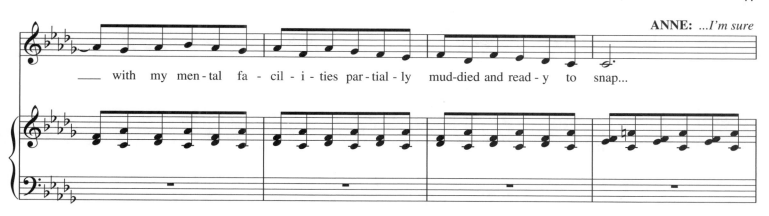

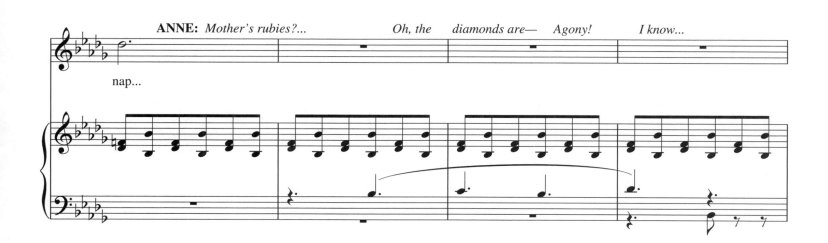

LATER

Music and Lyrics by
STEPHEN SONDHEIM

HENRIK:

Lat- er... When is lat- er?... All you ev - er hear is

"Lat- er, Hen - rik! Hen - rik, lat - er... Yes, we know, Hen - rik... Oh, Hen - rik...

Ev-'ry-one a-grees, Hen-rik... Please, Hen-rik!" You have a thought you're fair-ly burst-ing with, a

per-son-al dis-cov-er-y or prob-lem, and it's "What's your rush, Hen-rik? Shush, Hen-rik...

Good-ness, how you gush, Hen-rik... Hush, Hen-rik!" You mur-mur, "I on-ly... It's just that...

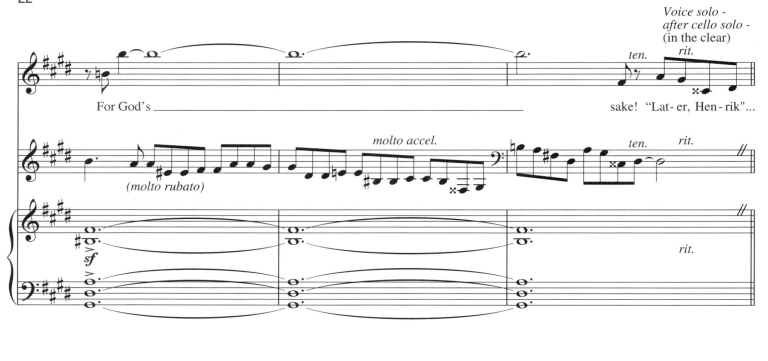

*Voice solo -
after cello solo -
(in the clear)*

For God's _____ sake! "Lat- er, Hen- rik"...

"Hen- rik"...   Who is "Hen- rik"?...   Oh, that law- yer's son, the

one who mum- bles... Short and bor- ing... Yes, he's hard- ly worth ig- nor- ing, And who cares if he's all

(looks up)
dammed—I beg your par-don—up in-side?　　　　　　As I've

of-ten stat-ed,　　It's in-tol-er-a-ble be-ing tol-er-at-ed.

"Re-as-sure Hen-rik, poor Hen-rik... Hen-rik, you'll en-dure be-ing pure, Hen-rik."

Though I've been born, I've nev-er been! How can I wait a-round for lat-er, I'll be

nine-ty on my death-bed and the late, or rath-er lat-er, Hen-rik Eg-er-man! Does-n't an-y-thing be-

gin?

A Little Night Music

SOON

Music and Lyrics by
STEPHEN SONDHEIM

This trio has been adapted as a solo for Anne.

Soon, _____ what - ev - er _____ you

say. _____ E - ven

a tempo *accel. poco a poco* *rit.*

now, _____ When you're close and we touch, _____

And you're kiss - ing my brow, _____

I don't mind it too much. _____

And you'll have to ad - mit I'm ___ en - dear - ing,

___ I help keep ___ things hum - ming, ___ I'm

not dom - i - neer - ing. _____ What's

REMEMBER?

Music and Lyrics by
STEPHEN SONDHEIM

This song is sung by the ensemble (Mr. Lindquist, Mrs. Nordstrom, Mrs. Segstrom, Mr. Erlansen, Mrs. Anderssen).

The ten - or on the boat that we char - tered, belch - ing "The Bar - tered Bride"... Ah, how we
The wine that made us both rath - er mer - ry And oh, so ver - y frank. Ah, how we

laughed, Ah, how we cried. Ah, how you prom - ised and
laughed, Ah, how we drank. You ac - qui - esced And the

Ah, how I lied. That di - lap - i - dat - ed inn—
rest is a blank. What we did with your per - fume...

Re - mem - ber, dar - ling? The pro - pri - e - tress - 's grin, Al - so her
Re - mem - ber, dar - ling? The con - di - tion of the room When we were

glare.
Yel-low ging-ham on the bed—
Re-mem-ber, dar - ling?

through...
Our in-ven-tions were u-nique,
Re-mem-ber, dar - ling?

And the can-o-py in red,
Need-ing re - pair? _____

I was limp-ing for a week; you caught the flu... _____

1

I think you were there. _____

I'm sure it was

2

you. _____

YOU MUST MEET MY WIFE

Music and Lyrics by
STEPHEN SONDHEIM

Tempo di Valse – (Slow 3)

FREDRIK:

This solo for Fredrik, presented here, continues in the show as a duet for Fredrik and Désirée.

Più mosso

hap-pi-est mis-take, The ache of my life: _____ You must meet my wife. _____ She bub-bles with pleas-ure, She glows with sur-prise, Dis-rupts my ac-cus-tomed lei-sure And ruf-fles my ties. _____ I don't know e-ven now quite how it be-

LIAISONS

Music and Lyrics by
STEPHEN SONDHEIM

Moderate 3

MADAME ARMFELDT:

At the vil - la of the Bar - on De Sig - nac, ____

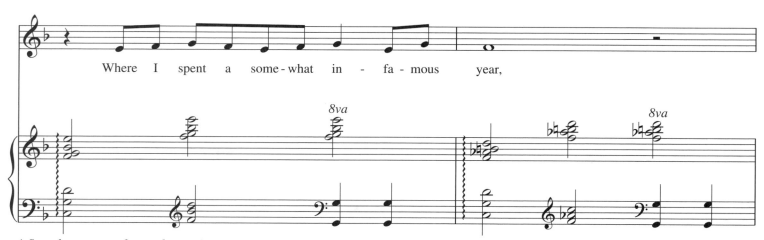

Where I spent a some - what in - fa - mous year,

* Sounds an octave lower than written.

now just a sim-ple lit-tle frock; What once was a sump-tu-ous feast is

Rubato

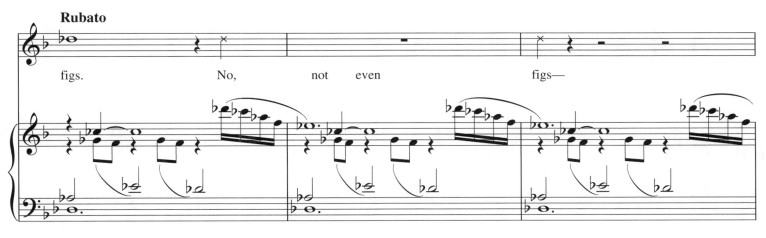

figs. No, not even figs—

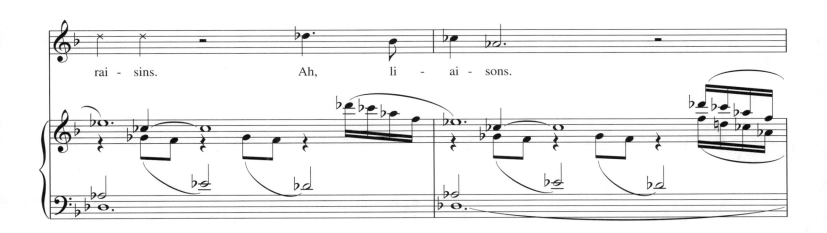

rai - sins. Ah, li - ai - sons.

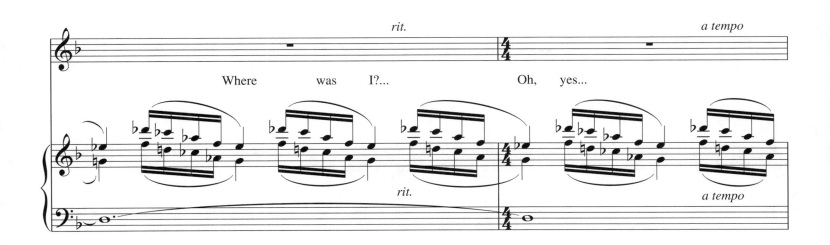

rit. *a tempo*

Where was I?... Oh, yes...

rit. *a tempo*

lack of taste that they dis - play.

Where is style? Where is

skill? Where is fore - thought?

Where's dis - cre - tion of the heart, Where's

pas - sion in the art, Where's craft?

With a smile And a will, But with

more thought, I ac -

quir - ed a cha - teau ex - trav - a - gant - ly o - ver -

staffed.   Too man - y

peo - ple mud - dle sex with mere de - sire,   And when e -

mo - tion in - ter - venes, the nets de - scend.   It should on

no ac - count per - plex, or worse, in - spire.   It's but a

pleas - ur - a - ble means to a meas - ur - a - ble end.

Why does no one com - pre - hend?

Let us hope this lu - na - cy is just a trend. *rit.* Where was I?...

a tempo Oh, yes... In the cas - tle of the king of the

Li - ai - sons to - day.

Un - ti - dy—__

Take my daugh-ter, I taught her, I tried my best to point the

way.

I e - ven named her Dé - si -

rée.

In a world where the

princ - es are law - yers,

What can an - y - one ex - pect ex -

cept to re - col - lect Li - ai...

IN PRAISE OF WOMEN

Music and Lyrics by
STEPHEN SONDHEIM

Tempo di Polonaise

CARL-MAGNUS:

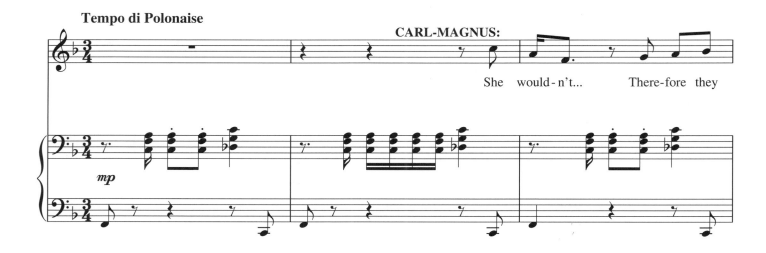

She would-n't... There-fore they

did-n't... So then it was-n't... Not un-less it... Would she? She

does-n't... God knows she need-n't... There-fore, it's not.

sign? ... What non-sense... He brought her pa-pers, They were im-por-tant so he had to be there. I'll kill him... Why should I both-er? The wom-an's mine! Be-sides, no mat-ter what one might in-fer, One

place. In - suf - fer - a - ble, yes, but gen - tle, Their weak-ness - es are in - ci -

den - tal. A func - tion - al but or - na - men - tal

Race. Du - ra - ble, sen - si - ble

wom - en... Wom - en... Ver - y near - ly in - dis - pen - sa - ble

EVERY DAY A LITTLE DEATH

Music and Lyrics by
STEPHEN SONDHEIM

(ANNE:) In the mur - murs, in the paus - es, In the ges - tures, in the sighs.

(CHARLOTTE:) In the but - tons, in the bread.

Ev - 'ry day a lit - tle dies

Ev - 'ry day a lit - tle sting

In the looks and in the lies,

In the heart and in the head,

A Little Night Music

NIGHT WALTZ

Music and Lyrics by
STEPHEN SONDHEIM

Tempo di Valse

The song is sung by the ensemble.

Ves - pers sound and it's six o' - clock, _____ Twi - light,

All a - round, But the sun sits

low, _____ As low as it's go - ing to

go. _____ Eight o' - clock, _____ Twi - light,

How en - thrall - ing, it's Nine o' - clock, _____ Twi - light,

Slow - ly crawl - ing towards Ten o' - clock, _____ Twi - light,

Crick - ets call - ing, The ves - pers

ring, _____ The night - in - gale's wait - ing to

sing. The rest of us wait on a

string. Per - pet - u - al sun - set is rath - er an

un - set - tling thing...

IT WOULD HAVE BEEN WONDERFUL

Music and Lyrics by
STEPHEN SONDHEIM

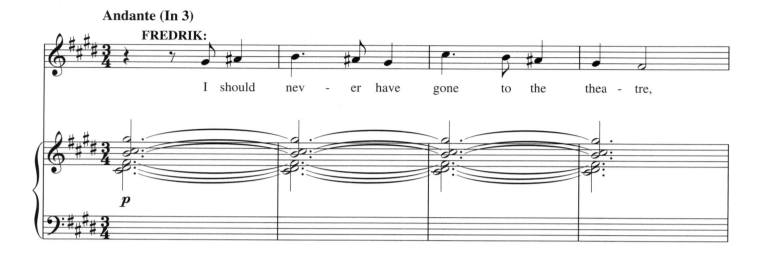

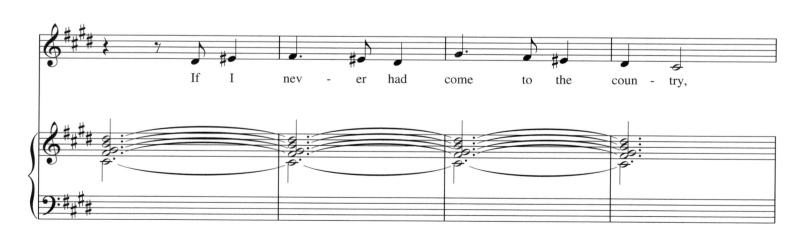

Mat - ters might have stayed as they were.

♩. = 100

CARL-MAGNUS: Sir.

FREDRIK: Sir.

(2nd time *pp*)

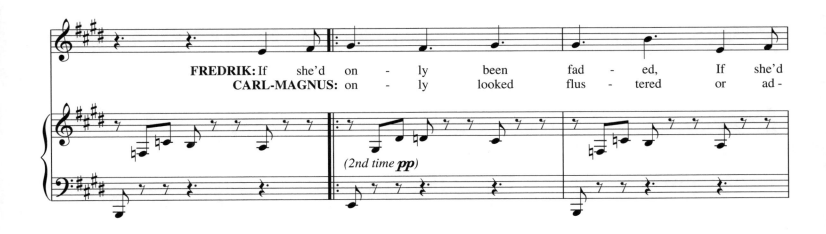

FREDRIK: If she'd on - ly been fad - ed, If she'd
CARL-MAGNUS: on - ly looked flus - tered or ad -

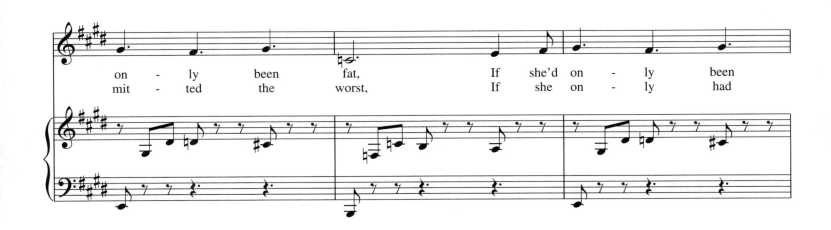

on - ly been fat, If she'd on - ly been
mit - ted the worst, If she on - ly had

lu - sive - ly cold, If she'd on - ly been bit - ter or, bet - ter, looked
start - ed to flinch, If she'd cried or what - ev - er a wom - an would

pass - a - bly old, If she'd been cov - ered with glit - ter or e - ven been
do in a pinch, If I'd been cer - tain she nev - er a - gain could be

cov ered with mold, It would have been won - der - ful. But the
trust - ed an inch, It would have been won - der - ful. But the

wom - an was per - fec - tion, To my deep - est dis -
wom - an was per - fec - tion, not an ac - tion de -

tear- ful...Or dead... It would have been won - der - ful. _____ But the

wom - an was per - fec - tion And the pros - pects are

grim, That love - ly per - fec - tion That

noth - ing can dim. Yes, the wom - an was per-

A Little Night Music

SEND IN THE CLOWNS

Music and Lyrics by
STEPHEN SONDHEIM

THE MILLER'S SON

Music and Lyrics by
STEPHEN SONDHEIM

THE GLAMOROUS LIFE
from the film version of *A Little Night Music*

Music and Lyrics by
STEPHEN SONDHEIM

Mend the clothes and tend the chil - dren. Or - din-ar - y moth - ers, like

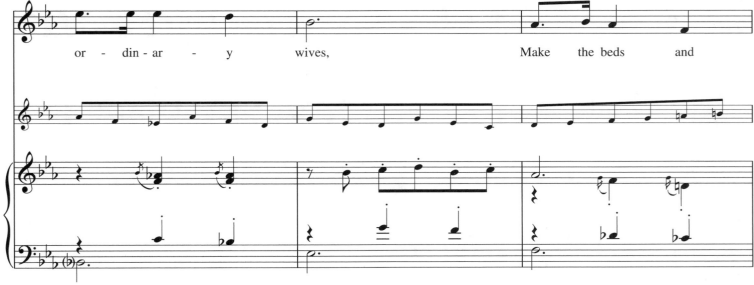

or - din-ar - y wives, Make the beds and

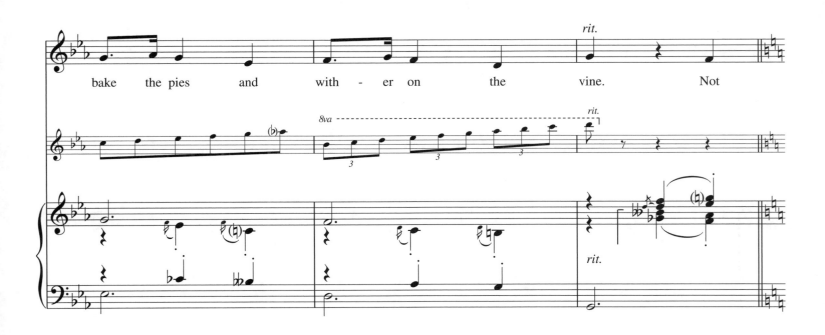

bake the pies and with - er on the vine. Not

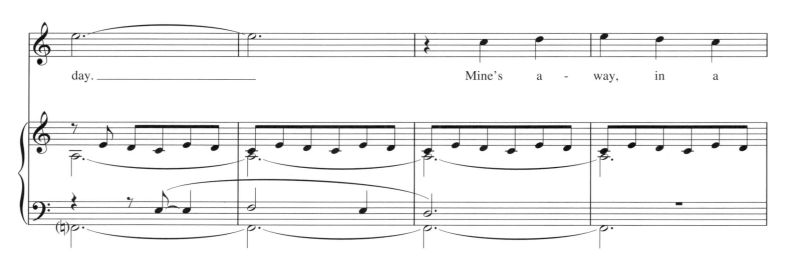

day. _____ Mine's a - way, in a

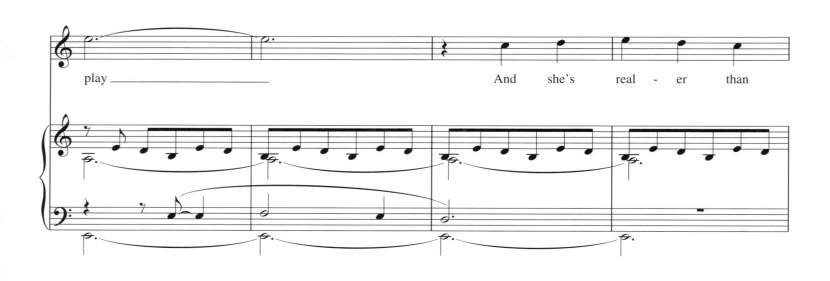

play _____ And she's real - er than

they. _____

She's in her king - dom, Wear - ing dis -

guis - es, Liv - ing a life that is full of sur -

pris - es. And

cresc.

cresc. poco a poco

some - time this sum - mer she'll come gal - lop - ing

sub. **p** *cresc. poco a poco*   *sim.*

thrill _____ Of the glam - or - ous

life! _____

stacc.

dim. poco a poco

molto rit.

p